First Printing, 2018
ISBN 978-1983718779

Mom and Daughter Journal

Fun, Prompted Journal to Get to Know your Teen Daughter Better

Catherine Adams

How to use this journal

Use the journal in the way that makes the most sense for you and your daughter. If she doesn't like to write, you can read and discuss the questions with her. If she enjoys writing, then you can take turns filling out the pages. If you need more space, there are blank pages in the back of the book or you can use additional sheets to expand on the questions.

If there are questions that don't apply or that either of you don't like...skip them! Feel free to jump around or take turns picking questions; there is no specific order to them and no need to do every one. The blank pages at the end of the journal can be used for you to come up with your own questions for each other.

I sincerely hope that you will be able to discuss your answers with each other, bond, and above all else, have fun!

My daughter and I are starting this journal

_____
(date)

My hope is that we will :

_____   have a little fun with it

_____   get to know each other a little
          better

_____   do a little bonding

_____   _____

I promise never to ask for more than 2
pages a day and I will let her skip any
pages she doesn't feel like doing.

_____
(sign)

Daughter - answer

I have agreed to try this journal because:

_____   my mom asked me to

_____   I appreciate that she wants to
get to know me better

_____   it sounds like fun

_____   _____

If we complete at least _____ percent
we will celebrate by:

_____

_____
(sign)

Mom - answer

Your daughter woke up this morning with one of the following traits. How will she rank which she would want to be?

_____ Stunningly Beautiful

_____ Crazy Smart

_____ Super Popular

_____ Wildly Talented

Optional: After you both have answered, discuss or write why you chose the traits you did or if you were surprised by each others choices:

_____
_____
_____
_____
_____
_____
_____
_____

You woke up this morning with one of the following traits. Rank them from 1- 4 which you would want to be:

_____   Stunningly Beautiful

_____   Crazy Smart

_____   Super Popular

_____   Wildly Talented

Optional: After you both have answered, discuss or write why you chose the traits you did or if you were surprised by each others choices:

_____

_____

_____

_____

_____

_____

_____

_____

_____

CONGRATULATIONS...
You are now the
Supreme Ruler of Earth
and you may solve one World Problem
today........What will it be?

_____ Disease

_____ War/Terrorism

_____ Climate Change & Pollution

_____ Poverty/Starvation

_____ Drug/Substance Abuse

Why? _____
_____
_____
_____
_____
_____

Daughter - answer

CONGRATULATIONS...
You are now the
Supreme Ruler of Earth
and you may solve one World Problem
today........What will it be?

_____ Disease

_____ War/Terrorism

_____ Climate Change & Pollution

_____ Poverty/Starvation

_____ Drug/Substance Abuse

Why? _____
_____
_____
_____
_____
_____
_____

Mom - answer

When you were little where was the scariest place in your room?

_____   Under the bed

_____   In the closet

_____   Outside the window

_____   Somewhere else?

What did you think was hiding? What did you think would happen? (write/share/discuss)

_____

_____

_____

_____

_____

_____

_____

_____

Daughter – answer

When you were little where was the scariest place in your room?

_____ Under the bed

_____ In the closet

_____ Outside the window

_____ Somewhere else?

What did you think was hiding? What did you think would happen? (write/share/discuss)

_____

_____

_____

_____

_____

_____

_____

_____

_____

Mom – answer

What 2 things are you the most worried about regarding your daughter right now?

_____

_____

What 2 things are you the most worried about regarding your daughter in the future?

_____

_____

Optional: After you both have answered, discuss or write why you chose your answers or if you were surprised by each others choices:

_____

_____

_____

_____

_____

_____

_____

Daughter – answer

What 2 things are you the most worried about right now?

_____

_____

What 2 things are you the most worried about in the future?

_____

_____

Optional: After you both have answered, discuss or write why you chose your answers or if you were surprised by each others choices:

_____

_____

_____

_____

_____

_____

_____

Mom – answer first

About School....

This year what subject does your daughter...

do the best in?

_____

like the most?

_____

like the least?

_____

find the easiest?

_____

find the hardest?

_____

Optional: After you both have answered, discuss or write if you were surprised by each others choices:

_____

_____

_____

_____

_____

About School....

This year what subject do you...

do the best in?

_____

like the most?

_____

like the least?

_____

find the easiest?

_____

find the hardest?

_____

Optional: After you both have answered, discuss or write if you were surprised by each others choices:

_____

_____

_____

_____

_____

Mom - can you draw ?

an umbrella

a cactus

a turtle

a ghost

Daughter - can you draw ?

an umbrella

a cactus

a turtle

a ghost

Mom – answer first

What are 2 ways you still treat your daughter like a little kid?

_____

_____

What are two ways you treat her like an adult?

_____

_____

Daughter - answer

Read what your mom wrote. Check the ones
you agree with. If you want to add different
things put them below:

_____

_____

_____

_____

Do you believe in ghosts? yes / no

Why or why not? (write or discuss)

_____

_____

_____

_____

_____

_____

_____

_____

Do you believe in aliens? yes / no

Why or why not? (write or discuss)

_____

_____

_____

_____

_____

_____

_____

Do you believe in ghosts? yes / no

Why or why not? (write or discuss)

_____

_____

_____

_____

_____

_____

_____

_____

Do you believe in aliens? yes / no

Why or why not? (write or discuss)

_____

_____

_____

_____

_____

_____

_____

Mom - answer

What 3 positive traits would describe your daughter?

What are 2 things she does that you appreciate?

Daughter - answer

What 2 positive traits would describe your mom?

What is 1 thing she does that you appreciate?

You are stranded on a deserted island for a year so you are stuck with the same meal every day. What would you choose in each food group? (you have water available)

Meat/Protein _____

Carb/Bread/ _____
Rice/Potato

Vegetable _____

Drink _____

Dessert _____

You are stranded on a deserted island for a year so you are stuck with the same meal every day. What would you choose in each food group? (you have water available)

Meat/Protein _____

Carb/Bread/
Rice/Potato _____

Vegetable _____

Drink _____

Dessert _____

Mom – answer

List 2 fun things you think your daughter should do more of:

_____

_____

List 2 fun things you should do more of:

_____

_____

Write about a special memory of something you did together? (write/share/discuss)

_____

_____

_____

_____

_____

_____

_____

_____

List 2 fun things you think your mom should do more of:

_____

_____

List 2 fun things you should do more of:

_____

_____

Write about a special memory of something you did together? (write/share/discuss)

_____

_____

_____

_____

_____

_____

_____

_____

_____

_____

YAY !!!
You just won a tattoo !!!
Are you happy or not?
(circle one)

What is it and where is it going?
(draw or write below)

YAY !!!
You just won a tattoo !!!
Are you happy or not?
(circle one)

What is it and where is it going?
(draw or write below)

Mom – answer

List 3 things you are proud of your daughter for this year:

_____

_____

_____

Optional: After you both have answered, discuss or write why you chose your answers or if you were surprised by each others choices:

_____

_____

_____

_____

_____

_____

_____

_____

_____

Daughter – answer

List 3 things you are proud of yourself for this year:

_____

_____

_____

Optional: After you both have answered, discuss or write why you chose your answers or if you were surprised by each others choices:

_____
_____
_____
_____
_____
_____
_____
_____
_____
_____

> Hola! Bonjour! Ciao!
> Namaste! Salaam!
> Ni Hau! Ola! Bula!

Your daughter woke up this morning fluent in a new language. What do you hope it is?

_____

Why?

_____

_____

What would you want it to be for yourself?

_____

Why?

_____

_____

Hola! Bonjour! Ciao!
Namaste! Salaam!
Ni Hau! Ola! Bula!

You woke up this morning fluent in a new language. What do you hope it is?

_____

Why?

_____

_____

What would you want it to be for your mom?

_____

Why?

_____

_____

Mom – answer first

What are 2 things you think you have done right in raising your daughter?

_____

_____

_____

_____

What is something you wish you had done better or different in raising your daughter?

_____

_____

_____

_____

What is one thing you could still improve on?

_____

_____

_____

_____

Read what your mom has written.

Place check marks next to the ones you agree with.

Place X's next to the ones you don't agree with.

What is one thing you will do the same in raising your children?

_____

_____

_____

_____

What is one thing you will do different in raising your children?

_____

_____

_____

_____

In your ideal job/career what has been the most important for you? Rank 1-7:

_____ Great location

_____ Rewarding/love it

_____ Lots of travel

_____ High income

_____ Great co-workers

_____ Lots of time off

_____ Makes a difference

Optional: After you both have answered, discuss or write why you chose what you did or if you were surprised by each others choices:

_____

_____

_____

_____

_____

_____

Daughter – answer first

In your ideal job/career what will be the most important for you? Rank 1-7:

_____ Great location

_____ Rewarding/love it

_____ Lots of travel

_____ High income

_____ Great co-workers

_____ Lots of time off

_____ Makes a difference

Optional: After you both have answered, discuss or write why you chose what you did or if you were surprised by each others choices:

_____

_____

_____

_____

_____

_____

Mom – answer

What are 2 ways men have life easier than women?

_____

_____

What are 2 ways women have life easier than men?

_____

_____

Optional: After you both have answered, discuss or write why you chose what you did or if you were surprised by each others choices:

_____

_____

_____

_____

_____

Daughter - answer

What are 2 ways men have life easier than women?

_____

_____

What are 2 ways women have life easier than men?

_____

_____

Optional: After you both have answered, discuss or write why you chose what you did or if you were surprised by each others choices:

_____

_____

_____

_____

_____

_____

Do you believe in guardian angels? yes / no

Why or why not? (write or discuss)

_____

_____

_____

_____

_____

_____

_____

_____

_____

Do you believe in miracles? yes / no

Why or why not? (write or discuss)

_____

_____

_____

_____

_____

_____

_____

_____

_____

Do you believe in guardian angels? yes / no

Why or why not? (write or discuss)

_____

_____

_____

_____

_____

_____

_____

_____

_____

Do you believe in miracles? yes / no

Why or why not? (write or discuss)

_____

_____

_____

_____

_____

_____

_____

_____

Mom – answer first

Which will your daughter think is better of the choices below?:

	City	Country	
	Kittens	Puppies	
	Marvel	D.C.	
	Vampire	Werewolf	
	Surprises	Planned events	
	Extra Credit	Curve	
	Running	Swimming	
	Winning $20	Finding $20	
	Free appetizer	Free dessert	
	Staying up late	Sleeping in late	
	Chocolate	Vanilla	
	Pink	Black	

Which of the choices below is better?

	City	Country	
	Kittens	Puppies	
	Marvel	D.C.	
	Vampire	Werewolf	
	Surprises	Planned events	
	Extra Credit	Curve	
	Running	Swimming	
	Winning $20	Finding $20	
	Free appetizer	Free dessert	
	Staying up late	Sleeping in late	
	Chocolate	Vanilla	
	Pink	Black	

Mom – answer

Circle the 3 life goals that you wish most for your daughter:

Being healthy

Having a successful career

Caring for others

Making the world a better place

Finding a life partner

Being rich

Having children

Being happy

Having close friends

Being famous

Exploring/Traveling

Optional: After you both have answered, discuss or write why you chose what you did or if you were surprised by each others choices:

_____

_____

_____

Daughter – answer

Circle the 3 life goals that you wish most for yourself:

Being healthy

Having a successful career

Caring for others

Making the world a better place

Finding a life partner

Being rich

Having children

Being happy

Having close friends

Being famous

Exploring/Traveling

Optional: After you both have answered, discuss or write why you chose what you did or if you were surprised by each others choices:

_____

_____

_____

In what way was your life easier at your daughters age than it is for her now?

_____

_____

_____

_____

_____

_____

_____

In what way was your life harder at your daughters age than it is for her now?

_____

_____

_____

_____

_____

_____

_____

_____

_____

In what way do you think your life is harder for you than it was for your mom at your age?

_____

_____

_____

_____

_____

_____

_____

_____

Optional: After you both have answered, discuss or write why you chose your answers or if you were surprised by her answers:

_____

_____

_____

_____

_____

_____

_____

_____

_____

Check 3 things you'd like to do more of with your daughter:

_____ cook together

_____ play games

_____ have conversations

_____ be active (walks/bike rides...)

_____ go out to lunch or dinner

_____ go to a movie

_____ play video games

_____ do crafts/art/projects

_____ _____

Optional: After you both have answered, agree to do at least one that you both checked sometime in the next week or two.

_____

_____

_____

Daughter – answer

Check 3 things you'd like to do more of with your mom:

_____ cook together

_____ play games

_____ have conversations

_____ be active (walks/bike rides...)

_____ go out to lunch or dinner

_____ go to a movie

_____ play video games

_____ do crafts/art/projects

_____ _____

Optional: After you both have answered, agree to do at least one that you both checked sometime in the next week or two.

_____

_____

_____

Which 3 qualities do you think your daughter needs most from you, especially during her teen years?

Encouragement	
Clear and consistent rules	
A sense of humor	
Listening without giving advice	
Genuine interest in activities	
Direction and guidance	
Setting a good example	
Open communication	
Unconditional love	
Understanding and forgiveness	

Optional: After you both have answered, discuss or write why you chose what you did or if you were surprised by each others choices:

_____

_____

_____

_____

_____

Especially during your teen years, pick the top 2 qualities you need most from your mom:

Encouragement	
Clear and consistent rules	
A sense of humor	
Listening without giving advice	
Genuine interest in activities	
Direction and guidance	
Setting a good example	
Open communication	
Unconditional love	
Understanding and forgiveness	

Optional: After you both have answered, discuss or write why you chose what you did or if you were
surprised by each others choices:

_____

_____

_____

_____

_____

Mom – answer second

In what two ways are you and your daughter the most alike?

_____

_____

In what two ways are you and your daughter the most different?

_____

_____

Optional: After you both have answered, discuss or write why you chose what you did or if you were surprised by each others answers:

_____

_____

_____

_____

_____

_____

In what two ways are you and your mom the most alike?

_____

_____

In what two ways are you and your mom the most different?

_____

_____

Optional: After you both have answered, discuss or write why you chose what you did or if you were surprised by each others answers:

_____

_____

_____

_____

_____

_____

Mom – answer first

What you say can sometimes be annoying. (hard to believe, I know). Check the ones you say on a regular basis. Check the two you think most annoy your daughter.

Mom says	say regularly	most annoying
How was school?		
When I was your age...		
Because I said so.		
Are you going to wear that?		
This is why we don't have nice things.		
You're still on that electronic?		
Don't you have any homework?		
You need to clean your room.		
Money doesn't grow on trees.		
You're just going though a phase		
add your own:		

Daughter – answer second

What your mom says can sometimes be annoying.
Check the ones that you hear on a regular basis.
Check the two that most annoy you.

Mom says	hear regularly	most annoying
How was school?		
When I was your age...		
Because I said so.		
Are you going to wear that?		
This is why we don't have nice things.		
You're still on that electronic?		
Don't you have any homework?		
You need to clean your room.		
Money doesn't grow on trees.		
You're just going through a phase		
add your own:		

Mom - answer

So...it turns out you get a super power on your 50th birthday. What do you hope it is?

_____ mind control

_____ invisibility

_____ super strength

_____ super speed

_____ fly

How will you use it?

_____

_____

_____

_____

After answering..were you surprised by each others choices? How?

_____

_____

_____

_____

So...it turns out you get a super power on your 20th birthday. What do you hope it is?

_____ mind control

_____ invisibility

_____ super strength

_____ super speed

_____ fly

How will you use it?

_____

_____

_____

_____

After answering..were you surprised by each others choices? How?

_____

_____

_____

_____

Do you believe in karma? yes / no

Why or why not? (write or discuss)

_____
_____
_____
_____
_____
_____
_____
_____

Do you believe in love at first sight? yes / no

Why or why not? (write or discuss)

_____
_____
_____
_____
_____
_____
_____
_____

Do you believe in karma? yes / no

Why or why not? (write or discuss)

_____

_____

_____

_____

_____

_____

_____

_____

Do you believe in love at first sight? yes / no

Why or why not? (write or discuss)

_____

_____

_____

_____

_____

_____

_____

_____

Mom – answer

You just won a time travel trip!

Do you want to go:

_____ to the past

_____ to the future

what period of time in the past or how far into the future?

_____

_____

What would you want to see or do?

_____

_____

After answering..were you surprised by each others choices? How?

_____

_____

_____

_____

You just won a time travel trip!

Do you want to go:

_____ to the past

_____ to the future

what period of time in the past or how far into the future?

_____

_____

What would you want to see or do?

_____

_____

After answering..were you surprised by each others choices? How?

_____

_____

_____

_____

Mom – answer

Do you think your daughter has ever...

	yes	no
Eaten a bug?		
Been in a physical fight?		
Been bullied?		
Had a crush?		
Lied about her age?		
Stayed up all night?		
Seen something illegal?		
Sent an e-mail or text by mistake?		
Gone skinny dipping?		
Hid something from you?		
Gotten away with something at school?		
Made a prank phone call?		
Been offered weed?		

When you're both done, check the ones on her side that are correct about you. Only do this if you can both handle the truth!

Do you think your mom has ever...

	yes	no
Eaten a bug?		
Been in a physical fight?		
Been bullied?		
Had a crush?		
Lied about her age?		
Stayed up all night?		
Seen something illegal?		
Sent an e-mail or text by mistake?		
Gone skinny dipping?		
Hid something from you?		
Gotten away with something at school?		
Made a prank phone call?		
Been offered weed?		

When you're both done, check the ones on her side that are correct about you. Only do this if you can both handle the truth!

Your daughter just won a **Vacation Home** that she can use every weekend. The perfect place would be...(check one in each group)

located

_____ on the oceanfront

_____ in the mountains

_____ by a lake

with a great view of the

_____ sunrise

_____ sunset

There would be plenty of

_____ outdoor activities

_____ indoor activities

and lots of

_____ quiet time

_____ parties

You just won a **Vacation Home** that you can use every weekend. The perfect place would be...(check one in each group)

located

_____   on the oceanfront

_____   in the mountains

_____   by a lake

with a great view of the

_____   sunrise

_____   sunset

There would be plenty of

_____   outdoor activities

_____   indoor activities

and lots of

_____   quiet time

_____   parties

Mom – answer first

Predict which of the following statements your daughter will agree with:

	agree	dis-agree
Celebrities earn too much money		
The death penalty should be eliminated.		
Military service should be mandatory.		
Most homework is a waste of time.		
Marriage is outdated.		
Animals shouldn't be used for research.		
Marijuana should be legalized nationally.		
Countries should have open borders.		
Everyone has a soulmate.		
The drinking age should be lowered.		

Daughter – answer

Do you agree or disagree with the following?

	agree	dis-agree
Celebrities earn too much money		
The death penalty should be eliminated.		
Military service should be mandatory.		
Most homework is a waste of time.		
Marriage is outdated.		
Animals shouldn't be used for research.		
Marijuana should be legalized nationally.		
Countries should have open borders.		
Everyone has a soulmate.		
The drinking age should be lowered.		

Mom – draw your daughter's favorite

fast food

sport to play

dessert

animal

Daughter – draw your mom's favorite

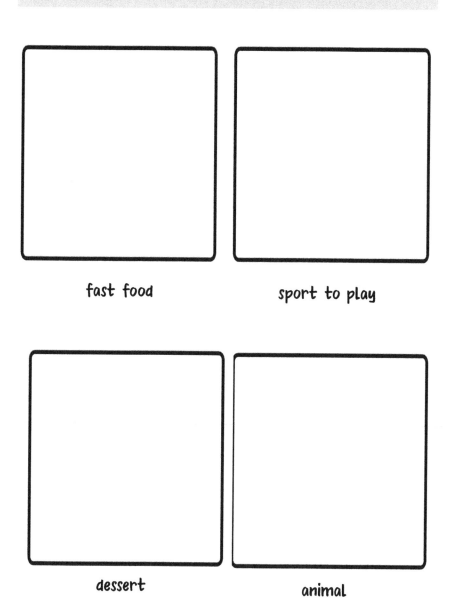

fast food

sport to play

dessert

animal

Check 3 things you hope your daughter knows:

_____ how much I love her

_____ what a great person I think she is

_____ how much I worry about her

_____ how much I believe in her

_____ how much I trust her

_____ how special she is

_____ how much I expect of her

Check 3 things you hope your mom knows:

_____ that I'm trying

_____ that there are a lot of pressures on me

_____ that I'm not an idiot

_____ that she can trust me

_____ that I'm not going to do anything really stupid

_____ that I need space to grow

_____ that I think about my future

Mom – answer

Question:
_____
_____
_____

Answer:
_____
_____
_____
_____
_____
_____
_____
_____
_____
_____
_____
_____
_____
_____
_____
_____

Daughter - answer

Question:

_____

_____

_____

Answer:

_____

_____

_____

_____

_____

_____

_____

_____

_____

_____

_____

_____

_____

_____

_____

_____

Mom – answer

Question:

_____

_____

_____

Answer:

_____

_____

_____

_____

_____

_____

_____

_____

_____

_____

_____

_____

_____

_____

_____

_____

Daughter – answer

Question:

_____

_____

_____

Answer:

_____

_____

_____

_____

_____

_____

_____

_____

_____

_____

_____

_____

_____

_____

_____

Mom – answer

Question:
_____
_____
_____

Answer:
_____
_____
_____
_____
_____
_____
_____
_____
_____
_____
_____
_____
_____
_____
_____
_____

Daughter - answer

Question:

_____

_____

_____

Answer:

_____

_____

_____

_____

_____

_____

_____

_____

_____

_____

_____

_____

_____

_____

Mom - answer

Question:

_____

_____

_____

Answer:

_____

_____

_____

_____

_____

_____

_____

_____

_____

_____

_____

_____

_____

_____

_____

_____

Daughter - answer

Question:

_____

_____

_____

Answer:

_____

_____

_____

_____

_____

_____

_____

_____

_____

_____

_____

_____

_____

_____

_____

_____

_____

Mom – answer

Question:

_____

_____

_____

Answer:

_____

_____

_____

_____

_____

_____

_____

_____

_____

_____

_____

_____

_____

_____

_____

_____

Daughter – answer

Question:

_____

_____

_____

Answer:

_____

_____

_____

_____

_____

_____

_____

_____

_____

_____

_____

_____

_____

_____

_____

_____

Mom – answer

Question:
_____
_____
_____

Answer:
_____
_____
_____
_____
_____
_____
_____
_____
_____
_____
_____
_____
_____
_____
_____
_____
_____

Daughter - answer

Question:

_____

_____

_____

Answer:

_____

_____

_____

_____

_____

_____

_____

_____

_____

_____

_____

_____

_____

_____

_____

_____

Made in the USA
Monee, IL
18 November 2019

17044681R00049